E 7 A

C000228378

Psalms

SONGS OF LIFE

CWR

John Houghton

Contents

Introduction

Open a printed Bible halfway through and you'll find yourself in the middle of the Psalms. Quite literally, the heart of the Scriptures is not a theological address nor a great historical event; it is passionate poetry.

These poetic prayers, or songs of life, express truth in a profoundly emotional manner that resonates with our universal human experience. The Psalms are full of theology, but it isn't systematic or carefully argued. These are not merely intellectual or academic compositions, but works of art that must be allowed to speak the truth, heart to heart and soul to soul. This is living and lived out theology applicable to any and every situation we may find ourselves in today.

The contents of the book of Psalms span about a thousand years from c. 1410 BC to c. 430 BC. Various people, most notably David, were involved both in writing and editing the five collections that comprise our biblical book of 150 psalms. Opinions vary concerning the divine inspiration of the titles given to some of the individual psalms. We will assume that where they refer to specific events, those psalms should be interpreted in the light of those events.

Although the psalms were composed during the old covenant period, they also hint at the new covenant that was to come. However, they are not written as allegories. Apart from where the New Testament allows us to draw parallels – for example, the king and the Messiah, Jerusalem and heavenly Jerusalem, the Mosaic covenant and the new covenant – it is it not necessary to make everything 'fit'.

The psalms are earthy and honest in addressing our frail and fallible human condition. In the light of an eternal living Creator they demonstrate what it is like to follow an

invisible God in a world full of idols. This is the life of faith. The composers know the reality of fear and doubt, being often surrounded by both spiritual and mortal enemies. They also experience the passionate love and mercy of God that fills them with joy and devotion. Sometimes confused and perplexed, other times triumphant and rejoicing, they invite us to join with them, to feel what they felt, and through that shared experience to learn the ways of the Lord. This is a journey through the rugged terrain of life, with its ups and downs, well-watered valleys and arid hills, its dangers and delights, its fears and failures, its temptations and triumphs. These are the authentic trials of all true pilgrims of faith, which is why they speak so powerfully and relevantly to generation after generation right up to our present time.

The psalmists pray honest prayers, sometimes outrageously so. They reflect on the greatness and sovereignty of the Creator and Lord of the nations; they bask in the love, mercy, forgiveness and kindness of their God. They experience genuine intimacy in their relationship with Him. In troubled times, facing opposition, danger and death, they cast themselves desperately on the Lord for protection and deliverance, and when they fall into pits of despair, frustration and confusion they complain furiously! Yet God's Word revealed through Scripture, nature and conscience is still their delight and they love to praise Him. They have hope, too. One day the Messiah will come and His judgment will bring justice to all the oppressed.

The psalms were commonly sung and accompanied by musical instruments ranging from the lone lyre to the full orchestra. A rhythmic, natural minor Mesopotamian scale probably prevailed, for these psalms were composed in the familiar poetic and musical genre of the day. The music was neither odd nor religious. Dance and bodily movement were used to express the natural unity of body and soul in response to God.

The poetic form is called Hebrew parallelism. These are rhymes that rely on related thoughts rather than the sound or word endings familiar in classical Western poetry. As a simple example take, 'Praise the LORD, my soul; all my inmost being, praise his holy name' (Psa. 103:1). The repeated thought intensifies the instruction, but it also tells us that 'soul' equals 'inmost being', and that 'his holy name' is what we mean by 'LORD' in this context. By using this form of poetry it is possible to translate the psalms into any language without loss of meaning. Psalm 119 is, additionally, an acrostic poem based on the 22 letters of the Hebrew alphabet.

To help us make sense of such a large book, we have identified seven dominant interwoven themes that will form the basis for our studies. Grouping the psalms under these headings is only approximate but it will provide an adequate framework for understanding all 150 songs. To prepare for the discussion starters, it will be beneficial to read the Bible readings suggested. For enhanced reading, you will find listed all the psalms appropriate to the theme in the Leader's Notes at the back of this guide. To this end all group members might like to obtain their own copy of the book as it will also serve as a useful reference for personal future reading of the Psalms.

All the psalms are suitable for meditation and group study, and many are suitable for normal church worship – more than our contemporary songwriters perhaps allow. Our prayer is that this series of studies will inspire a greater connection with the whole of life in our worship expression, so that the Psalms may more fully become the songbook of the Church.

WEEK ONE

Psalms of Education

'The fear of the LORD is the beginning of wisdom' (Psa. 111:10)

Opening Icebreaker

How would you illustrate to a child the difference between data, knowledge and wisdom?

Bible Readings

- Psalm 1
- Psalm 25:8–15
- Psalm 50:7–15
- Psalm 91
- Psalm 111
- Psalm 115:2–8
- Psalm 127

Opening Our Eyes

Our first selection of psalms emphasises the importance of learning wisdom. It is a relatively rare commodity among the young, and often lacking in the old. No one can earn a certificate in wisdom. Rather than an academic qualification or position in society, it is how we actually live that reveals whether we are wise or foolish. That is why these psalms urge us to pursue wisdom as a way of life and not just as a religious activity. Wisdom is the learned art of exercising godly common sense. It may not seem very exciting, but the psalmists took great delight in acquiring it. So let's look deeper.

Wisdom has much to do with perspective. Time-driven as we are, we can too easily react impulsively and unwisely: think about impulse buying, impatient aggressive driving, passing on unverified gossip, the angry outburst. A rash investment is seldom wise; nor is going along with the crowd or the daily news headlines. But 'The fear of the Lord' helps us to see life from His eternal point of view.

Proverbs contrasts wisdom with folly (Prov. 8:1–9:12). In the Psalms it is also contrasted with wickedness. There is no 'love the sinner; hate the sin' in these poems. Not all people are wilfully wicked, but the wicked sin because they are wicked (Psa. 50:16–21). Evil actions spring from unclean hearts (Matt. 15:11,17–20) and false wisdom. Even in the covenant nation of Israel, circumcision had to be of the heart and not just the body (Deut. 10:16; 30:6). James takes the same radical line, urging us to reject the false and pursue true wisdom (James 3:13–18).

These wisdom psalms turn the focus away from ourselves and onto God. Knowing our mortality, we do not presume to negotiate self-gratifying deals with our almighty Creator

(Psa. 49:6). This is what distinguishes the righteous from the wicked. It is knowing God authentically in the centre that produces an ethical lifestyle, not the other way around (Psa. 127:1–2). Ours is a stressed, guilt-ridden, anxious and insecure society, yet so much of modern life is a futile attempt at self-salvation. We try the latest meditation course to ease our stress. A new diet promises a sense of ethical wellbeing that adds to our self-worth. A religious routine, a course of study, a sports regime, supporting humanitarian projects, political engagement – these may be worthwhile activities in themselves, but they will not save our souls.

These psalms teach us that the wisest thing we can ever do is acknowledge our follies, call on the Lord for forgiveness, and submit to His will. This is the path to redemption, transformation and peace. It produces a humble life of ethical integrity that demonstrates the wisdom of the Lord's ways. We enter God's protection. We discover that He has advice for every aspect of our lives – work, family, leisure, finance, friendship and church. This is God's way of integrated living and He promises to prosper us in it, not simply because we 'asked Jesus into our hearts' but because we daily commit our way to Him.

Let's abandon our popular image of the wise man or woman. This is not a call to become a solo guru living on a higher plane than everyone else. True wisdom is expressed not in lofty pronouncements but in everyday participation in our communities of family, work, leisure and church.

Discussion Starters

1. Reading Psalm 1, what do you think are the characteristics of a wise, ethical lifestyle? Discuss examples in modern life.

2. Guilt is commonly recognised as the number one factor causing stress and mental illness. From reading Psalm 25, what are the benefits of confessing our sins to God? How would you encourage someone else to do so?

3. Psalm 115 contrasts the living God with idols. What are the idols of our age? How do we avoid idolatry?

4. Psalm 91 offers a life of supernatural protection. How do we obtain this?

5. Psalm 50 tells us we cannot trade with God by sacrifice or service. He owns everything; He needs nothing. What are the two things He encourages us to do instead?

_____

_____

_____

_____

6. Psalm 111 emphasises that God is a God of revelation. He speaks through creation, covenant and conscience. Share experiences of God speaking to you.

_____

_____

_____

_____

7. Psalm 127 teaches us the wisdom of integrated living. What does this mean in practice?

_____

_____

_____

_____

Personal Application

Wisdom is not a matter of finding a Bible text for every decision, let alone applying random verses to every tiny particular instance in life. Rather, wisdom springs from a heart that is comfortable in God's presence without any division between the sacred and the secular. Wise people come across as incredibly normal and friendly. They do not act oddly or religiously.

Take time this week to review the various aspects of your life in the light of God's Word and wisdom. Reflect on your work, family, leisure, finances, relationships and church. Are there any adjustments you would make? Could you discuss this with those close to you?

Seeing Jesus in the Scriptures

Psalm 40:7-8 teaches us that Jesus came full of God's Word and delighting to do His will. Yet that will did not start when He reached 30 years of age. Luke 2:42,52 records that from the age of 12 onwards Jesus grew in wisdom and favour. For the next 18 years that wisdom was expressed in helping run the family business, providing for their needs using His own skilled hands, playing His part in village life, and attending the local synagogue.

This firm foundation in everyday life provided the launching pad for His three years of astounding ministry that went on to change the course of world history. His wise teaching continues to inspire and direct us, but it is not simply for our education. His dynamic Spirit is equipping us to sow His wisdom into every aspect of modern life.

WEEK TWO

Psalms of Consolation

'I will fear no evil, for you are with me' (Psa. 23:4)

Opening Icebreaker

Share brief stories of personal scary moments in your lives.
How did you cope? Did God intervene in some way?

Bible Readings

- Psalm 27:1–3
- Psalm 37:1–10
- Psalm 42
- Psalm 56
- Psalm 62:1–8
- Psalm 121
- Psalm 141

Opening Our Eyes

Life presents us mortals with some serious challenges and few of us get through entirely unscathed by one kind of trouble or another. Certainly, Jesus offered no assurances of a pain-free life for His followers; indeed, He told us to expect the same sort of treatment the world gave Him (John 15:20; 16:33) and this is along with sharing the common human weal of living in a fallen creation. Things go wrong, and as much for believers as for anyone else.

Overt persecution is minimal in the West, but in many parts of the world it means living under the real threat of violence, oppression, deprivation and even death. It is widely recognised that Christianity remains the most persecuted faith on earth. Spiritual warfare is not optional in the Christian life. We may opt timidly to hide our light under a bucket or stoically to brave it out, but neither approach is a good example of liberating, glorious faith in action.

This selection of psalms suggests another way. We can recognise the unavoidable reality of the spiritual battle (2 Tim. 3:12), but then take comfort and strength from the far greater reality of God's love, presence and power in our lives. We don't pretend that 'the wicked are not really that bad'. We know they are – and so does God. It is evil that will fail in the end, not goodness. That much is certain. Our Creator never sleeps; He is always on guard, so we can sleep in peace even in the midst of troubles. Nor will He ever abandon us to an untimely death.

The psalmists (eg Psa. 3:5; 23:4–5; 27:1–3) have discovered that it is possible to live free from fear and intimidation in an age of anxiety and uncertainty, even when God sometimes seems slow to act, or even completely silent. Our consolation – our comfort and confidence – does not lie with politicians or in military might, nor yet in amassing great defensive wealth. We do not look to these 'hills', but to the Lord who made heaven and earth. He is our rock, our fortress and our deliverer. He is our shield and defender.

This is not to say it is always easy. There is mystery in God's will; time and circumstances do take their toll on us. This journey includes valleys of suffering and we, like the psalmist, can be honest about our doubts and difficulties. Yet we can discover, too, the reality of our faith and enter His spiritual protection plan. Faith triumphs through the trial, not by avoiding it.

The outcome is certain: God will vindicate His people (Psa. 135:14). He, and they, will be exalted among the nations. Discovering this, the psalmist determines to maintain his personal integrity. He will not yield to compromise because he knows that he is under the Father's loving protection. Whatever the challenges and mysteries of life and suffering, whatever the anxiety and confusion all around us, we may be confident that behind it all God is outworking His redemptive purposes. We might feel isolated in our pain; it may seem strange that we 'must go through many hardships to enter the kingdom of God' (Acts 14:22), but that doesn't mean anything is wrong. Indeed, it may well be evidence that we are getting it right. So, we should keep to the path that, through all the ups and downs and twists and turns, leads surely to God's dwelling place. And whether we feel it or not, His presence is always with us.

Discussion Starters

1. From reading Psalm 27:1–3, what do you consider to be the secret of inner peace?

_____

_____

_____

_____

2. Reflecting on Psalm 56, how might you advise people who are being abused, bullied or threatened?

_____

_____

_____

_____

3. From looking at Psalm 121, what does it mean to hope in God our Creator?

_____

_____

_____

_____

4. Difficult times can persist. What consolation can we find from Psalm 62?

_____

_____

_____

_____

5. Nostalgia can paralyse us for the present and make
    the future appear bleak. What does Psalm 42 say is
    the antidote?

    _____

    _____

    _____

    _____

6. 'Why do "evildoers" prosper?' is a perennial question for
    faith. What answers do we discover from Psalm 37:1–10?

    _____

    _____

    _____

    _____

7. The world is full of temptations to compromise our faith
    and conduct. What does Psalm 141 encourage us to do?

    _____

    _____

    _____

    _____

Personal Application

Psalm 116 is a good example of the life, death, resurrection pattern that is intrinsic to our existence, as it was for Jesus: 'I was dying, I prayed, God saved me. Be at peace, soul!' None of us likes the dying aspect, but in Christ it is redemptive (see John 12:23–26). The chick growing in the egg needs the discomfort to make it break out of the shell into fuller life.

Reflect on how past sufferings, healthily embraced, have brought you closer to the Lord and provoked spiritual growth. The psalmist's testimony of hope and consolation is found in Psalm 118:17–18,24. May it be ours, also.

Seeing Jesus in the Scriptures

Psalm 23 is not just for funerals! Jesus is the good shepherd (John 10:11–18). He is our consolation in life, not just in death. This is our story: Because the Lord is my shepherd I do not lack peace, refreshment or guidance. I do not fear dark valleys because He is with me. He blesses me when I am beleaguered, and promises me lifelong goodness and mercy, and an eternal home.

Rejoice in Him, tell Him your woes, doubts and fears, let Him direct your steps, and thank Him for His amazing provision and deliverance. Perhaps the greatest consolation of all is the awareness of His presence in even the toughest of times. 'Peace I leave with you; my peace I give you. I do not give to you as the world gives. Do not let your hearts be troubled and do not be afraid' (John 14:27).

WEEK THREE

Psalms of Exasperation

'I cried out to God for help; I cried out to God to hear me.'
(Psa. 77:1)

Opening Icebreaker

Take it in turns to share one trivial issue that winds you up,
and one serious issue of social or ethical injustice that stirs
your Christian conscience.

Bible Readings

- Psalm 7:6–9
- Psalm 28
- Psalm 35
- Psalm 43
- Psalm 55:16–23
- Psalm 58
- Psalm 142

Opening Our Eyes

Is it all right to become frustrated and exasperated with God – and to say so? This largest set of psalms (see Leader's Notes) expresses, with ruthless honesty, exactly how we sometimes feel about our lot in life and the injustices meted out to the poor and vulnerable. They are not usually the psalms we want to sing in a church service, but they do give us a healthy permission to let our guard down before God and not to bottle up our feelings. We may rant and scream at Him if we wish. Outrageous events should outrage us. We can be angry without sinning (Eph. 4:26) when confronted by blatant abuse, political and social injustice, and religious persecution. 'Why are you silent, God? How much longer do we have to put up with this pain? Why do the innocent suffer?' These are the legitimate complaints of troubled believers.

More honesty? These so very human saints pray even vindictive prayers: 'I hate these evildoers and I want them dead! Give them a taste of their own medicine. They brutally slaughtered our children. Do the same to theirs! Wipe out their family line. See how they like it!'

Such honesty is healthy – certainly better than repression – and it may relieve our anguish and stress better than sedatives, but it is only a step on the journey, not the destination. If it were, we would be left bitter and cynical, and false guilt over our outbursts might leave us feeling so bad, so sinful, that we struggle to find peace again.

Recognising this, these psalmists do not set out to avenge either themselves or to do so on behalf of the persecuted. In accord with Paul's later counsel (Rom. 12:17–21), they call on God to do the avenging and then leave it to Him. This is truly radical; it is the way of Christ Himself (1 Pet. 2:21–23). The truth is, only God sees the full picture. Our limited human perspective flaws our strongly felt judgments. Experience will teach us that the Lord has His own ways of dealing with evil, and in any case, no 'evildoer' will ultimately escape His justice. Nor are we necessarily blameless ourselves. The world doesn't divide neatly into oppressed and oppressors. All of us need the grace, mercy and forgiveness found in Jesus.

The next step in dealing with our exasperation is one reached in almost all of these psalms. It is to express hope and trust in the Lord. In spite of everything, *God is still good*, and getting all the pain out of our system allows us to see that afresh. Everything may appear to be so wrong, but God's love and goodness continues to undergird His creation. We can still trust in His unfailing love. He remains our fortress, our refuge and our hope. He has heard our cry for mercy, even if we don't think so.

We may not understand the reasons why people endure so much suffering, but we do know that God works everything according to His good will and in His good time. So let us not withdraw into our pain. Instead, let's rejoice with His people: our tongues proclaim His righteousness and praise. We can say, 'Cheer up, my soul! Hope in God. I will praise Him, my Saviour and my Lord, for He is just and will judge properly. Despite everything, I will sing my praises to Him and declare His righteous acts.'

Discussion Starters

1. It is perfectly legitimate to plead our own innocent cause and ask for justice. Discuss what this means using Psalm 7.

2. Using Psalm 58, discuss how we could judge politicians properly.

3. The desire for vengeance, for justice, is understandable, but it belongs to God, not us. What do you make of the honesty of Psalm 28?

4. There is systematic corruption in high places as well as low. How could we respond to unrighteous rulers, employers, and local government? See Psalm 35.

5. When we are persecuted for righteousness sake, what does Psalm 55 enable us to learn?

_____

_____

_____

_____

6. Weariness with evil and oppression can depress us. What is the remedy found in Psalm 43?

_____

_____

_____

_____

7. It's not wrong to complain about our situation before God but He doesn't want us to stay there. How might we find a way forward? See Psalm 142.

_____

_____

_____

_____

Personal Application

When under personal trial, Paul encourages us to bless our persecutors (Rom. 12:17–21). And, wherever we can, let's aim to alleviate the plight of the poor and oppressed. However, when facing overwhelming need, these psalms encourage us to vent our honest feelings. Artists and poets do this using their creative gifts, but all of us can try writing our personal psalms of exasperation. Why not try this now?

Having done so, commit the matter to the Lord's justice and find peace in the pain. Hope in God. Ultimately, we cannot lose, because He cannot lose. One day He '"will wipe every tear from their eyes. There will be no more death" or pain, for the old order of things has passed away' (Rev. 21:4). So let's praise Him, whatever!

Seeing Jesus in the Scriptures

People who do evil often appear simply to evade justice when they die. Human justice seems cheated. But divine justice is not. Jesus is the God-appointed judge of the living and the dead (2 Tim. 4:1). Only those whose names are in His book of life are spared (Rev. 20:11–15). In Revelation 6, the age-old cry for justice rises to God, and the wrath of the Lamb falls on the politicians and military leaders, and slaves and free alike. This is justice day when Christ both judges the raging nations, and rewards His prophets, saints and worshippers (Rev. 11:17–18). The King and Lord of all is battle-ready to execute the final judgment that ends all corruption. The psalmists' cries for justice are at last answered and exasperation gives way to exaltation.

WEEK FOUR

Psalms of Anticipation

'Your throne, O God, will last for ever and ever' (Psa. 45:6)

Opening Icebreaker

Ask group members to talk about an event that they were eagerly anticipating, and share how they felt when that event arrived.

Bible Readings

- Psalm 21
- Psalm 45
- Psalm 72
- Psalm 89:1–4
- Psalm 129
- Psalm 132:10–18

Opening Our Eyes

A royal thread of promise runs throughout the Old Testament. One day, a Spirit-anointed and God-appointed king will arise. His reign will last forever and will be established over all nations. Israel is the chosen, though unlikely, vehicle to usher in this reign. By the time we reach the Psalms the focus has sharpened to the line of David. God made a permanent covenant with him and his descendants to fulfil this Messianic role. The language used is a complex interweaving of both the earthly reign of David, that of his descendants, and the Messianic reign (see my guide in this same series, *The Covenants*, pp35–40).

At first, David's successor, Solomon, appeared to meet all the ideals, but it soon ended in tears. The kingdom split in two, and the era of being ruled by kings ended in the disaster of the Babylonian captivity. Apart from the brief period of the Maccabean rulers (c. 167–37 BC), and the Herodian puppet kings under the Romans (c. 37 BC – AD 100), the nation was from then on dominated by pagan empires. Today, Israel is nationally a secular democracy.

However, the Messianic promise remained alive. Mostly couched in nationalistic terms, there were those who saw a greater, spiritual dimension to the promise. In these Messianic psalms we have to tease out the latter from the former in the light of the advent of Jesus of Nazareth.

When Jesus appeared, He confounded Messianic expectations, first because He did not arise from within the ruling hierarchy, and second, because His vision extended way beyond Jewish nationalism. Even worse, He was executed by the occupying Roman power. As a nationalistic king, Jesus failed. In fact, it appeared that He had no interest in fulfilling that Messianic interpretation, and was intent on redefining what it really meant in the hearts and minds of His followers.

Jesus Himself and the apostles demonstrate that He did fulfil all the Messianic prophecies in the Old Testament, including those in the psalms we are studying. He performed many miracles, He spoke a powerful prophetic message, and incontrovertibly He rose from the dead. Now ascended to the Father, He rules the nations. So, why the controversy?

Jesus had a clear intent behind His teaching. He seldom made His identity explicit, because He was looking for faith within His hearers, for the enlightenment of the Holy Spirit, for evidence of spiritual understanding. These are the characteristics of those whom the Father is calling. These are the ones who recognise His kingship and call Him Lord. They live as citizens of heaven under a heavenly reign. By their lives and testimony, they extend that reign on earth in the same manner that He did. By faith.

The story of the King is far from over. 'God exalted him to the highest place and gave him the name that is above every name, that at the name of Jesus every knee should bow, in heaven and on earth and under the earth, and every tongue acknowledge that Jesus Christ is Lord, to the glory of God the Father' (Phil. 2:9–11). That this mission of God challenges the powers that be, both spiritual and earthly, goes without saying. Jesus paid the price to accomplish redemption for us all. Following Him still means being despised, hated, misunderstood by a world that nonetheless wants the blessings that He offers. Yet Jesus will return to complete the Messianic mission and usher in a renewed heaven and earth. That is the heart of Christian hope.

Discussion Starters

1. Jesus rose from the dead. He also ascended to heaven as Lord of all. From reading Psalm 21, what does this mean for world history?

_____

_____

_____

_____

2. From studying Psalm 89, in what ways is God's promise for an endless king fulfilled in Jesus?

_____

_____

_____

_____

3. What does it mean that Jesus is a king after the order of Melchizedek (Psa. 110:4)?

_____

_____

_____

_____

4. From reading Psalm 72, what are the implications of the Messiah's reign for the poor and oppressed?

_____

_____

_____

_____

5. Psalm 129 is a Messianic prayer reminding us that Jesus' life was not easy or popular. What bearing on the cost of discipleship does this have for us?

_____

_____

_____

_____

6. Psalm 45 celebrates the King and His Bride. What response does that evoke in you?

_____

_____

_____

_____

7. What do we learn about how God wants His Church to behave from looking at Psalm 132?

_____

_____

_____

_____

Personal Application

Psalm 2 teaches us that God will tolerate no nonsense from the arrogant rulers of this world. He has appointed His Son as the risen and ascended Christ. He rules over the nations from the reality of His heavenly Jerusalem. This is an established fact, not wishful thinking. God has served the governments and peoples of this world with due warning: yield to His reign or be shattered!

We are ambassadors for Christ, called to treat all people as He would – with humility, love and grace – but to do so confidently and unashamed, as bearers of good news. Whoever calls on the name of the Lord will be saved. From that moment on, people with no previous qualifications begin to live and to operate under the politics of heaven.

Seeing Jesus in the Scriptures

Psalm 22 speaks prophetically of Jesus' sacrificial death. It reveals Him at His most vulnerable; the religion, the Romans and the rabble have all rejected Him. Even God has left Him as Jesus does the will of God. It is an alien, incomprehensible experience; hell itself. Drained and dislocated, torn by the 'wild animals' who crucify Him, stripped bare, rendered powerless and friendless, the Saviour dies for us all.

There is victory in the cross as well as apparent defeat. The Father does hear Jesus' cry; the suffering is not in vain. The devil is defeated. Salvation is accomplished for the whole world. People across the globe will draw near and worship Him as their vindicated and risen Lord. Sing hallelujah!

WEEK FIVE

Psalms of Lamentation

'The LORD has heard my cry for mercy; the LORD accepts my prayer.' (Psa. 6:9)

Opening Icebreaker

Share examples of incidents where God has brought good out of a bad situation and you can, in retrospect, thank Him for His grace towards you.

Bible Readings

- Psalm 38
- Psalm 41
- Psalm 51
- Psalm 85
- Psalm 102:1–3
- Psalm 106

Opening Our Eyes

It is often noted by social commentators that we live in a death-denying society. This makes these psalms particularly difficult. Some churches seem to be relentlessly upbeat in their corporate worship, perhaps to avoid the embarrassment of having to confront grief or pain; so they celebrate life now and don't brood on death and the afterlife. One consequence of this denial of mortality in our society is high levels of stress, anxiety, guilt and fear caused by unresolved grief.

Another issue that some churches struggle to know how to address is inappropriate relationships; ignoring or denying a difficulty exists instead of sensitively coming alongside those who may need guidance. This is how Jesus dealt with the woman at the well (John 4:7–26) and the woman caught in the act of adultery (John 8:2–11). In fact, our Lord was scandalous in His reception, care and restoration of those deemed 'unfit' for church.

There are, thankfully, many churches that do allow an opportunity for the confession of sins and to pray for those suffering and grieving. Even so, these psalms of lamentation take us to a deeper, more felt, level. They enable us to face the discomfort of grief and failure, to sing sad songs for sad days.

But let's not limit grief and sorrow simply to someone's death. Divorce causes grief, as does any broken friendship or relationship. Likewise injury, loss of a limb, disability, loss of health, even the ageing process itself involves sadness and grief. Redundancy, failing an exam or driving test, not obtaining the university place, flunking an interview, losing a race, being dropped from the team, all involve personal loss. More acute may be the plight of the refugee, or the rough sleeper, many of whom have lost everything.

Guilt is not simply individual, either. Isaiah cried out, 'Woe to me... I am ruined! For I am a man of unclean lips, and I live among a people of unclean lips' (Isa. 6:5). Sadly, the Church at large has much to lament for its failings, be that erroneous theology, neglect of the poor, misconduct and compromise, lack of spirituality, complacency, or divisiveness. As members of that worldwide Church, we cannot simply distance ourselves from all this. All Israel went into captivity, including the good guys. Humble corporate repentance is required of us all.

Lamentation is good for the soul. Drowning our sorrows, tranquillising the pain, projecting guilt onto others, going into denial, resolves nothing. It simply drives the sword of grief deeper where it causes further injury and infection. These psalms encourage us to pour out our souls before God, to confess our sins to Him, to weep out the pain and find healing for our guilt and grief. None of us should fear this, for God is a God of compassion who comforts us and forgives sins. Remember the life, death and resurrection pattern? He brings good out of evil. The process may take a while, it may involve forgiving as well as receiving forgiveness, giving comfort as well as receiving comfort. However, most of us who have made this journey would say in retrospect that we are better for it in ways we could never have imagined at the time.

Discussion Starters

1. Some, in Christian circles, may have encountered an unreal avoidance of bereavement and of grief over sin. What may be a healthy approach to facing up to these aspects of life? See Psalm 6 for an honest song.

2. Psalm 85 is a prayer of restoration. What do you think it means when it speaks of righteousness and peace 'kissing' (v10)?

3. Sickness can cause us to reflect on our life and mortality. How does Psalm 38 assist us in so doing?

4. Psalm 51 is the definitive psalm of repentance from serious sin. What was David's underlying sin and what do we learn from this?

5. It is very easy in our individualistic society to address only our own sins, God's people have had a chequered history. Looking at Psalm 106, what sins might tempt us and what do we need to ask God for?

_____

_____

_____

_____

6. How do we empathise with and help those who are enduring total disaster in their personal lives, such as refugees, rough sleepers, and runaway children? See Psalm 137.

_____

_____

_____

_____

7. We all must face our mortality, and the slow process of bereavement as our powers fade. Psalm 102 teaches us how to lament the passing years. Discuss how we can apply this to our ageing society.

_____

_____

_____

_____

Personal Application

Psalm 41 helps us to be honest with ourselves and to deal with regrets for our past errors that have caused trouble. There is always hope in God. Are there unresolved sins, particularly involving broken relationships, that you need to address? Are there pains that you have never perceived to be 'bereavements'? These may show up in your life as unfinished business, barely concealed regrets and sadness, nagging reminders that may disable you even today.

Like the psalmist you may find it helpful to express these issues, maybe writing your own prayers. Begin by just letting the feelings come out unedited as they will. Gradually, these disjointed thoughts and feelings will hopefully come together into prayers, which is where the deep healing begins.

Seeing Jesus in the Scriptures

Psalm 130:3–4,7–8 speaks of hope in God, the promise of forgiveness, redemption and restoration. Jesus came into the world to save sinners. He understands sorrow and bereavement; He experienced grief and wept. His comfort not only comforts us but also transforms our losses into a healing ministry for others (2 Cor. 1:3–5). The victims become the healers!

Our High Priest is not an aloof, distant, judgment figure (Heb. 4:15–16). Mercy is freely offered without recrimination. And 1 John 1:9 promises forgiveness and cleansing to all who draw near with an honest and humble heart. It is this ministry of accessible compassion that drew all the unlikely and 'unsuitable' people to Jesus. He hasn't changed.

WEEK SIX

Psalms of Contemplation

'Be still, and know that I am God' (Psa. 46:10)

Opening Icebreaker

Share your regular devotional practices with one another.
Do you have a regular pattern? What do you try to achieve in
those times?

Bible Readings

- Psalm 65
- Psalm 84
- Psalm 92
- Psalm 97
- Psalm 105:5–8,42–45
- Psalm 139:1–18

Opening Our Eyes

Mindfulness, meditation, and contemplation are practices that have come back into fashion. The growing popularity of these disciplines comes in response to the stress of modern life and the need to create mental and emotional space. As therapeutic practices they have considerable value, but the spirituality is often likely to be Buddhist or Hindu inspired, having to do with the emptying of the mind or emotions, or even allowing spirits to possess the psyche.

Christianity has a long contemplative tradition, but the difference is that it is mind *renewing* rather than mind *emptying*. In the process we realign ourselves with the reality of a living God, the rhythm of creation, and our redemption in Christ. We let the Holy Spirit breathe through our being. Instead of peace and stillness being the goal, peace is the blessed by-product of experientially focusing on the living truth.

There is no set method or time span for Christian contemplation; some prefer a liturgical approach following a fixed pattern each day; others find a 'sacred space', which may be anywhere without distraction. Some of us walk or run a familiar route, or go to an art gallery or place of natural beauty. Not building contemplation into our daily lives leads to becoming increasingly out of kilter with God. Little wonder we grow anxious, stressed and irritable in body, mind and spirit.

God has built Sabbath rest into creation so that we may uncouple from our daily burdens of work. However, all days need mini Sabbaths, rest periods during the daily round. The psalmists sometimes used the word 'Selah', which may be paraphrased as 'pause at this point and think about it'. This set of psalms urges us: 'Be still, and know that I am

God' (Psa. 46:10). As we step out of the rush of preoccupying thoughts and focus on the Lord and His voice, we will experience a heightened awareness: we will see more clearly and hear His voice better.

A number of these contemplative psalms focus on God's creative power. They remind us that He is not an app on a smartphone but the living Lord of the universe – an awesome God, indeed! When the psalmists confront the politics, the news headlines of the day, they do so in the light of God's justice. No government in a fallen world is wholly just and although we may lobby for change, our real battle is a spiritual one. Contemplating this leads us to understand what it means when Paul says 'God raised us up with Christ and seated us with him in the heavenly realms in Christ Jesus' (Eph. 2:6).

Life is full of decision-making and we are quite right to plan for the future. However, we are also mortal. It's a balance between fearful uncertainty and over-optimistic presumption. Meditating on this balance is good for the soul, reminding us that our lives are a gift from an immortal God.

How often do we praise God for His Church, despite its faults? The psalmist contemplated the wonder of Zion, the earthly focus of God's presence. The Church is the global manifestation of God's presence today and the instrument of Christ's on going ministry. These psalms also remind us of our own salvation history and the great adventure of His pilgrim people of whom we are part.

Meditating on the goodness of God reminds us that we are never alone or out of His thoughts.

Discussion Starters

1. Discuss why you think the psalmists often focus on the power of God revealed in creation (eg Psa. 97). What two effects might this have on us?

    _____
    _____
    _____
    _____

2. Corruption in government is endemic across the world. Since this is a spiritual issue (Eph. 6:12; 2 Cor. 10:3–5), from looking at Psalm 76 how do we exercise spiritual authority to establish God's reign?

    _____
    _____
    _____
    _____

3. Psalm 39 encourages us to choose life, but also contemplate our mortality. Discuss how we balance our life force and our mortal frailty.

    _____
    _____
    _____
    _____

4. Psalm 84 invites us to meditate on the glorious global ministry of the Church. Discuss what you think is wonderful about God's people.

    _____
    _____
    _____
    _____

5. Psalm 65 reminds us of our origins and how the Lord called us, redeemed us, and provided for us. Share some of the blessings of salvation with one another.

_____

_____

_____

_____

6. Psalm 105 reminds us that history matters to God's people. Why is this so important for our perspective on the Church?

_____

_____

_____

_____

7. Psalm 139 encourages us to contemplate the goodness of God. Discuss how we cultivate this awareness of His presence in our daily lives.

_____

_____

_____

_____

Personal Application

These psalms challenge us not simply to fit in a rushed
Bible reading, but to spend time meditating on the Lord
and His deeds. Wandering thoughts are actually welcome
provided we rehearse them before Him. They may help to
focus our prayers. Giving ourselves a prolonged time of quiet
contemplation in His presence will help us cope with the
troubles of our age.

What is your personal routine? It is helpful to think about
Bible passages in order to increase our understanding, but
what God loves most is for us to spend time in His presence
and listen to what He might say to us. Depending on our
circumstances, this isn't always easy to achieve, but it's
always worthwhile.

Seeing Jesus in the Scriptures

Jesus knew the value of silent time with His Father. He
understood that the busier we are the more we need to
contemplate. This is why Jesus would retreat to a deserted
place, and why He found praying during the night
worked best.

This was the secret of how He could fulfil His mission to do
only what He saw and heard the Father doing (John 5:19–20).
He listened. There was nothing automatic about this. Certainly
in His humanity Jesus had to walk the walk of faith and hear
His Father's will, step by step. Whatever the questions this
raises, we can at least conclude that if the Son of God needed
to spend quiet time with the Father, then most certainly
we do too.

WEEK SEVEN

Psalms of Adoration

'I will exalt you, my God the King; I will praise your name for ever and ever.' (Psa. 145:1)

Opening Icebreaker

Go around the group and, in as few words as possible, share why you love to praise the Lord.

Bible Readings

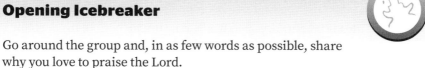

- Psalm 30
- Psalm 47
- Psalm 68:4–10,19–35
- Psalm 75
- Psalm 147
- Psalm 100

Opening Our Eyes

It is impossible to be a true believer and not also be a worshipper. This final set of psalms is all about the praise and thanksgiving that lies at the very heart and soul of faith. 'How lovely is your dwelling-place, LORD Almighty! My soul yearns, even faints, for the courts of the LORD; my heart and my flesh cry out for the living God' (Psa. 84:1–2). To praise and worship alone or with others is surely the most delightful and desirable of activities.

However, corporate worship can degenerate into mere repetition and routine, whatever our church tradition or style of music. Old songs are not necessarily venerable; nor do they always have better theology. Nor are new songs always better, either in words or music. True worship must spring from passionate Spirit-inspired hearts.

Jesus taught very specifically on worship both in the Sermon on the Mount (Matt. 6:5–18), and in discussion with the Samaritan woman (John 4:19–24). In the first instance, He challenged the hypocrisy of performance worship. We may all get caught up in the desire to impress people with our prayers and exhortations so they become little more than self-fueling hype. Even fasting can be made to look pious. By contrast, Jesus gives us a pattern of prayer – and, by extension, worship – that is God-centred, and firmly earthed in the reality of our hearts and lives. He teaches us to do our praying and worshipping out of the spotlight. This is how we receive the Father's blessing.

Speaking with the Samaritan woman, Jesus addresses the issue of holy places. Recognising that although the Samaritans had gone astray in establishing an alternative site to Jerusalem's Temple, He now announces a new understanding of worship. The focus is no longer on sacred spaces and worship centres. True worshippers do so 'in Spirit and in truth'. By implication, this means we can and should offer worship anywhere and everywhere and at all times. It also means that we worship as those inspired by the Holy Spirit of God and not from the energy of the self. Such worship is also in accord with the truth of God's revelation, and is offered with full integrity of heart.

These psalmists understood this, basing their exhortations to worship firmly on the acts and character of God. Considering what Jesus said, the Jerusalem Temple is now declared redundant and we focus instead on the heavenly temple, Jerusalem above. Revelation 4–5 gives us a timeless idea of what that is like. The focus is on the throne of God and the Lamb. He is the worthy one who has conquered; He has ransomed us for God, and He now rules the cosmos. It is a triumphant celebration that engages the Church, the angels, the spiritual powers, in fact, every created being throughout the universe. Who would even dare to draw attention to themselves?

Worship in the psalms was never simply cerebral; it embraced the whole body, not just the intellect. Worshippers leap and dance, they raise their hands and clap, they kneel and prostrate themselves, they shout for joy and make loud music, they sing and proclaim, and they invite all of creation to do the same. If truth is worth believing then it is worth celebrating with all our hearts, and that includes our bodies!

Discussion Starters

1. Psalm 30 gives us a number of reasons to praise the Lord. Discuss how they apply today.

2. In Psalm 47, the psalmist calls for noisy vibrant praise and worship to celebrate King Jesus' victory. How willing are we to praise Him loudly?

3. Psalm 68 celebrates the deliverance of God's people. How does this apply both in our personal lives and in relation to the persecuted saints across the world?

4. How can we keep informed and celebrate when churches and organisations obey the great commission to spread the good news of Jesus around the world?

5. Mostly the day of judgment is welcomed in the Bible because it puts right all the injustice and evil in the world. Psalm 75 invites us to incorporate this aspect into our worship. How can we do that?

_____

_____

_____

_____

6. Psalm 147 teaches us to celebrate the Lord's creative acts, and His redemptive acts. What are these acts an expression of?

_____

_____

_____

_____

7. Psalm 100 focuses on worshipping God. Given that 'church' does not mean a building in the New Testament, what does it mean to 'Enter his gates' (v4)?

_____

_____

_____

_____

Personal Application

A fundamental human sin is to refuse to give thanks to the Lord, and to worship created things rather than the Creator (Rom. 1:21–23). We believers are called to 'give thanks in all circumstances' (1 Thess. 5:18). So let's express our gratitude for the countless blessings that the Lord grants us every day.

Psalm 136 is an antiphonal (two parts alternating) psalm based on the many great reasons to celebrate God's enduring love. We often seek God with a list of needs; how about personalising this psalm to create a list of reasons to celebrate His love?

Seeing Jesus in the Scriptures

We know that Jesus was a worshipper during His time on earth, beginning with His family's regular attendance at the synagogue and their custom of going up to Jerusalem for the feasts.

When the 72 followers Jesus sent out on mission returned to record their successes, Luke accounts, 'At that time Jesus, full of joy through the Holy Spirit, said, "I praise you, Father, Lord of heaven and earth, because you have hidden these things from the wise and learned, and revealed them to little children. Yes, Father, for this is what you were pleased to do"' (Luke 10:21).

Paul writes in Hebrews 2:12: 'He [Jesus] says' "I will declare your name to my brothers and sisters; in the assembly I will sing your praises."' Let's follow Jesus' great example and be encouraged to praise and worship our heavenly Father, for He is most worthy of our adoration.

Leader's Notes

Week One: Psalms of Education

Focus: Pursuing wisdom results in right living.

I hope that, as leader, you will be thoroughly blessed leading these studies on the book of Psalms! Commence this session by reading the Introduction aloud. This will help orientate your group. Then continue to the Icebreaker. This is simply to get your group discussing the difference between data (information), knowledge (learning), and wisdom (godly life skills).

Have the members of your group read aloud the selected Bible Readings between them, then follow that with the Opening Our Eyes section. This will be the normal pattern for each session.

Discussion Starters

Each Discussion Starter is designed to help us grasp how wisdom applies to the different aspects of our lives.

1. Wisdom springs from who we are. See also Psalm 15. The psalmists draw a line between the upright and the ungodly. The fruitfulness of the former is revealed in personal integrity, a gentle tongue, and the absence of slander, gossip or malice. It means giving honour to the honourable but despising vile behaviour, in keeping one's word even when it costs, and in not making money out of other people's need, or accepting bribes.

2. See also Psalm 32. Guilt leads to anxiety and stress, but it arises initially from foolish life choices. Confession is not just good for the soul; it also benefits the mind and the body. People may pray their confessions but, if it helps, also write them out as a private prayer.

3. All idolatry is an attempt to fill a human need in a foolish manner. Dead themselves, idols only bring spiritual death to their worshippers. Todays idols include consumerism, addictive habits, and self-worship. See also Psalms 33, 49 and 53.

4. Psalm 91 contains a series of awesome promises. God will protect those who wisely place their lives under His care. Psalm 34:7,11,17–19 also give us great confidence in doing God's will.

5. It is not wise to bargain with God. Salvation is by grace alone. Mere religious activity cannot save. Instead, God looks for a thankful heart and a life without malice. Wisdom is gracious and compassionate. See also Psalms 82 and 112.

6. See also Psalm 119. This is an acrostic poem based on the 22 letters of the Hebrew alphabet; each verse contains a reference to delighting in and obeying God's revelation of His will through His Word.

7. Integrated living means a life of faith that has no secular compartments. Family life, daily work, fellowship with colleagues, friends and neighbours, can be as much an act of worship as a church service. See also Psalms 128, 133 and 146. You might like then to read the Seeing Jesus in the Scriptures section to remind your group what integrated living meant for Him.

Conclude this session by reading the Personal Application. With many false ideas about what wisdom or a wise person looks like, it is good to remember that living wisely should ideally be incredibly normal and unselfconscious. This section also invites us to perform a personal life review over the coming week. You may wish folk to feed back on what they learnt as a result of this. Some may prefer not to because their review involves other people or matters of a sensitive nature, so tread carefully and wisely.

If you're able to delve further into the book of Psalms we recommend reading the psalms below prior to your group meeting together. Some members of your group may wish to do the same. This way you will not simply have covered the content, but you will have imbibed some of the spirit and emotion of the psalms too.

Enhanced reading: Psalm 1; 15; 25; 32; 33; 34; 49; 50; 53; 81; 82; 91; 101; 107; 111; 112; 115; 119; 127; 128; 133; 146.

Week Two: Psalms of Consolation

Focus: Inner peace is the gift of the Lord.
Follow the same pattern as the previous week, reminding people of the suggestions for enhanced reading, which they may be able to complete in the week prior to each study.

Opening Icebreaker
Keep this one fairly light. Stories may include scary driving incidents, health threats, being trapped, losing track of your children... Encourage the focus to be on times when the Lord intervened either directly or through someone else.

Discussion Starters
1. People long for inner peace in our stressed out society. Is there any alternative to social, medical or illegal drugs to dull the pain? See Psalms 3, 11, 31 and 131. In a time of deep family stress, David found his peace in prayer. God would be his shield and that enabled him to sleep well. He set his priorities on God's presence and His will, not putting faith in worthless alternatives, nor fretting

about matters beyond him. It's a lesson for us when we let rumour, the news and matters beyond our control obsess us.

2. Bullying is cowardly and harassment is actually illegal in some forms in the UK. It continues because people fear worse consequences if they report it. Bullying can overwhelm the victim's whole life, but the psalmist insists on a heavenly perspective that will see divine justice done. God will vindicate the victims. Fear Him; bullies are mere mortals. Cry out before Him, but rise to a place of trust. See also Psalm 16, 20, 61 and 86.

3. See also Psalm 124. Hoping in God our Creator means lifting our eyes above the circumstances. David inhabited a violent neighbourhood. He was peacemaker among troublemakers, and he hated it. But help was not to come from the higher political or military powers. It would come from the Lord of heaven and earth, and He would protect His people.

4. See also Psalms 57 and 120. David was a refugee from political oppression, living with violent outlaws. Nevertheless, he insisted on praising the Lord for His great love and faithfulness. Troubles can be persistent, but we can discover a place of rest. However vulnerable we look, we are surrounded by God's invisible armour.

5. See also Psalm 46. Nostalgia is a dangerous indulgence when things are going badly. Reliving the good old days can so depress that it paralyses us into inaction. Yet our God gives us a future and a hope. We need to address our own souls and urge ourselves to put our hope in God for the future. The world seems chaotic, but God's Church remains. He has the future in hand and will bring an end to the anarchy.

6. See also Psalms 16 and 73. It's about perspective again. God's noble people inhabit the land; they are blessed and kept secure in the Lord. So don't fret; trust in God and do good. The meek will inherit the earth and the proud will vanish away. Stick with it; live as a faithful believer and see God's favour.

7. See also Psalm 5 and 125. It is easy to go with the crowd, to compromise our behaviour. Temptation is subtle and real, so the psalmist prays for protection and clear-sightedness about sin. Wickedness will only rule if God's people compromise. Since our tongues are hard to tame the psalmist prays to guard his mouth from compromised speech or deceptive delicacies. He will remain committed to God's safe path.

Read the Personal Application to help your group grasp the life, death, resurrection pattern of the Christian faith, and to rejoice in it because it is the pathway of salvation. Finish with the Seeing Jesus in the Scriptures section to remind us that Jesus is our good shepherd. You may wish to conclude with prayer for members of your group and beyond who are facing particular struggles.

Enhanced reading: Psalm 3; 5; 11; 16; 20; 23; 27; 31; 37; 42; 46; 56; 57; 61; 62; 73; 86; 116; 118; 120; 121; 124; 125; 131; 141.

Week Three: Psalms of Exasperation

Focus: Honest frustration before God is healthy, but justice belongs to Him alone.

Follow the same pattern as the previous week, encouraging people to read next week's enhanced reading in advance.

Opening Icebreaker

This is, at one level, a chance to share minor issues like, 'He/she always leaves the lid off the toothpaste.' At another level, members of your group may be seriously concerned about the plight of refugees, or child slave labour, or sex trafficking, or persecuted Christians.

Discussion Starters

1. See also Psalm 17 and 26. A righteous cause may be our own innocence. Despite legal safeguards, justice is not always done. For example, an employee can be falsely victimised and lose their job. Nonetheless, we must be sure that God finds us innocent, and that requires personal integrity.

2. Politicians can be judged by their party values and manifestos. Do these commit to the oppression of minorities, for example? How does their professed moral conduct stand up to examination? Do they uphold justice? Do they serve the people or exploit the electorate? Do they always tell the truth?

3. In the Garden of Gethsemane, Peter took the law into his own hands and earned the Lord's rebuke. It is right to call on God to punish the wicked and restrain evil, but not to make ourselves judge, jury and executioner. Evil has a habit of backfiring. It's called divine justice. Those who live by the sword will die by the sword. We may want seven times vengeance but God will repay justly. See also Psalms 10, 64 and 79,

4. Supernatural protection is promised to the oppressed. Believers do get killed, but there are many more miraculous interventions than ever reach the news. Let us not forget that He is the living God who is active in His world on behalf of His people. Psalm 83 addresses

a military confederacy aligned against Israel. See also Psalms 12, 13, 14, and 94.

5. See also Psalms 4, 44, 52, 54, 59, 69, 70, 71, 109 and 143. Real persecution costs the lives of countless Christians across the globe and deprives millions more of peace and freedom. This is no small issue and is both local and systematic. In one way or another it is always religiously motivated; it has to do with truth, and it has a satanic source. The fear is real, but so is the faith. The persecuted need our prayer and support to find divine deliverance. May those who persecute God's people find their violence recoils on themselves!

6. Trials can persist a long time and they can weary us. We must daily renew ourselves by hoping in God. He has a plan that will surely unfold. It is good to reflect on the history of God's previous acts. He hasn't changed! Tenacity is only developed through trial and testing. See also Psalms 60, 77 and 88.

7. See Psalms 123, 140 and 142. Our way forward from despair, deprivation and defeat is to turn our eyes to the Lord. Having told Him about our circumstances, we should then focus on the Lord of our circumstances. Setting our hope in God is the secret of character growth. Where are our eyes focused?

Read the Personal Application and encourage your members to try expressing their frustrations in word or song or picture. These may be for themselves or on behalf of others. This provides us with a tangible way of entering into these psalms for ourselves. End with the Seeing Jesus in the Scriptures section. This is about a perhaps unpopular theme – the judgment of God. It is something not to fear but to rejoice in. Almost all scripture relating to judgment has to do with vindicating God's people.

Enhanced reading: Psalm 4; 7; 10; 12; 13; 14; 17; 26; 28; 35; 43; 44; 52; 54; 55; 58; 59; 60; 64; 69; 70; 71; 77; 79; 83; 88; 94; 109; 123; 140; 142; 143.

Week Four: Psalms of Anticipation

Focus: Jesus is the true Messianic King.

Again, lead with the same pattern as the previous week. Also, following the Enhanced reading below, we have listed the Psalm references of prophecies about Jesus followed by the New Testament references of how they were fulfilled. If you have time you could have your group members read them out. There are many more in other parts of the Old Testament.

Opening Icebreaker

This icebreaker in intended to turn our thoughts towards what anticipation feels like. To avoid the repetition of wedding days or the birth of children, suggest choosing one that no one else has already chosen.

Discussion Starters

1. Psalm 21 (see also Psa. 24) speaks prophetically of the resurrection and exaltation of Jesus. Even though not everyone has yet acknowledged it, His reign has already begun (Heb. 2:8–9). The book of Revelation consists of a series of dramatic metaphors that help us explain what that reign implies. Don't try to fit it into a chronological sequence or match it to the current world scene. More important is to know that history is going somewhere and Jesus is in charge (Rev. 4:11–5:14).

2. Psalm 89 records, through the life of David, the covenant God has made with His eternal Son. Jesus is the Son of David, the fulfilment of this vow. David was mortal and God's blessing seemed to fail. What then of the covenant?

Similarly, Jesus appeared to fail but in fact triumphed. God remained true to His word promised to David. His kingdom has no end.

3. In Psalm 110, the name Melchizedek confuses some people. It means king of righteousness and refers back to an incident in Abraham's life (Gen. 14:18–20). Distinct from the time-bound Levitical priesthood, Jesus is a permanent priest, without beginning or end. This is the priesthood of the new covenant that supersedes the old and guarantees our eternal redemption in Christ who offered the perfect once-and-for-all sacrifice of Himself. See also Hebrews 5:6–10; 6:20.

4. Psalm 72 reminds us that divine justice is biased towards the powerless because they are most commonly exploited by the rich and powerful. A good ruler ensures equity for his people; a bad one exploits them. Solomon ultimately failed but Jesus never does. When the vulnerable are cared for with dignity we see evidence of Jesus' reign.

5. See also Psalm 40. These two psalms record David's discovery that bringing in God's reign was not easy. Misunderstanding, vested interests, jealousy and resentment all made his path hard. Jesus experienced the same resistance and opposition to His ministry. Instead of ploughing fields, they ploughed His back with furrows of pain. It is not likely to be easy for us either.

6. Psalm 45 is an acclamation to the King; a wedding song, no less, that reminds us of the anticipated marriage supper of the Lamb (Rev. 19:7–8; 21:1–2). Jesus loves His Bride, the Church, 'the new Jerusalem', and she is also honoured in this psalm.

7. Psalm 132 expresses David's desire to build a house for God. Zion is His chosen dwelling place, but David will not build it. That task will fall to Solomon. Sadly the subsequent temples did not see the glory of God until Jesus entered Herod's Temple. By then it was corrupted by moneymaking and business dealing. Jesus, full of zeal, insisted that church is about prayer and worship, not trade (John 2:13–17). We need to ensure that we keep to God's intent.

Read the Personal Application to remind the group that the love of God is also just. As our Creator, He has every right to insist that we obey His will. However, He still leaves our future dependent on us making wise choices of submission to His will. Finish with the Seeing Jesus in the Scriptures section. This is a good moment to ponder the mystery of the cross and to express our thanksgiving and praise.

Enhanced reading: Psalm 2; 21; 22; 24; 40; 45; 72; 89; 110; 129; 132.

Psalms fulfilled in the New Testament by Jesus: Psalm 2:7 (Matt. 3:17); 8:6 (Heb. 2:8); 16:10 (Mark 16:6–7); 22:1 (Matt. 27:46); 22:7–8 (Luke 23:35); 22:16 (John 20:25–27); 22:18 (Matt. 27:35–36); 34:20 (John 19:32–33,36); 35:11 (Mark 14:57); 35:19 (John 15:25); 40:7–8 (Heb. 10:7); 41:9 (Luke 22:47); 45:6 (Heb. 1:8); 68:18 (Mark 16:19); 69:9 (John 2:17); 69:21 (Matt. 27:34); 109:4 (Luke 23:34); 109:8 (Acts 1:20); 110:1 (Matt. 22:44); 110:4 (Heb. 5:6); 118:22 (Matt. 21:42); 118:26 (Matt. 21:9).

Week Five: Psalms of Lamentation

Focus: Expressing godly sorrow for sin and loss is the path to recovery.

Opening Icebreaker

This icebreaker assumes that your group now has a measure of confidence in one another. Be aware that though you should encourage the sharing of resolved issues, in the process some might realise that their issue is not as resolved as they thought. This is where pastoral sensitivity is necessary.

Discussion Starters

1. Ecclesiastes 3:4 tells us there are times to weep and mourn as well as times to laugh and dance. See also Ecclesiastes 7:2 and Psalm 6. Rather than anaesthetising ourselves against grief and failure, we should encourage honesty in our worship and in our fellowship. In the context of the life of devoted worship, Paul advocates fellowship in suffering – Romans 12:15.

2. Psalm 85 tells us that God listens. He can change our desperate state and forgive our sins. In Him failure is not final. But we still need restoration. God will speak peace but let us not return to folly. Righteousness and peace kiss at the cross. Whatever our past failures the Lord can grant us a good future.

3. This psalm is an honest acknowledgement of our mortality. Here we have a cry for mercy triggered by sickness and the fear of dying. In this case, the psalmist considers that sin has made him ill. His festering wounds are evidence of his overwhelming guilt. He is exhausted, depressed and his back hurts. People are already writing his obituary. His one hope lies in God's presence.

4. Psalm 51 was David's response to God after Nathan had confronted him with his sin. David had committed gross injustice against Bathsheba, against her husband, and against his whole army, but he recognised that his sin was ultimately against God alone. So to God he turns to seek forgiveness, to be washed clean. (Hyssop was a form of disinfectant.) Though by nature he was a sinner, he begs for a pure heart and a faithful spirit. What he offers is not payment but a broken and contrite heart.

5. God's people are to be salt and light but often we have lost our saltiness and the light wavers. It is small comfort, but we have a long history of failure. It doesn't excuse us, but it does remind us that God doesn't give up on His people. Like every other generation we need forgiveness.

6. In 586 BC, the Babylonians razed Jerusalem to the ground and deported its people. Everything familiar was destroyed and they were in total trauma. Many could not get their heads around it. Why had this happened? How had they not heard Jeremiah's passionate call for repentance? Their faith was wrecked and they could only mourn in an unfamiliar land. We have a responsibility to receive the alien the homeless and refugee and help them practically to rebuild their lives. See also Psalm 74.

7. The psalmist is confronting his mortality. Life is brief. Age has made him a shadow of his former self. His desire is for the restoration of God's people and he wants to live long enough to see it. God is eternal but the universe will wear out. We need God to teach us to number our days and be wise.

Read the Personal Application. The practical suggestion is a way of uncovering the truth about ourselves before God and is a well-tried way of unblocking the channels. Even if you can't think of anything to write, then write that! Finish with the Seeing Jesus in the Scriptures section to encourage the group that He is always open to our humble prayers for help and healing.

Enhanced reading: Psalm 6; 38; 41; 51; 74; 80; 85; 102; 106; 130; 137.

Week Six: Psalms of Contemplation

Focus: Contemplation time is a vital aspect of following the Lord.

Churches might use traditional or alternative methods to allow for times of contemplation. Both are valid ways for meditating on God's truth and presence. It's good to distinguish between the New Age self-help therapies and our need to realign our minds to God's reality, which brings its own therapeutic benefits. This accords with Paul's counsel in Romans 12:1–2.

Opening Icebreaker

Without making anyone feel guilty, share ideas for finding time and space to be still in God's presence. Discuss the benefits of regular contemplation.

Discussion Starters

1. See Psalms 8, 19, 29, 76, 93, 104 and 144. Meditating on the dramatic power of God revealed in creation reminds us of our powerlessness before Him. The fear of God is an appropriate response, just as we should fear a nuclear furnace. He is not our plaything. That awesome power also teaches us that He is well able to take care of His people.

2. Avoid getting distracted by party politics or local news. Justice is a global issue and its resolution is a matter of spiritual authority. The judgment of God, the ministry of Jesus, is about restoring justice to the oppressed and dealing with the oppressors. Behind these, lie the spiritual 'principalities and powers'. See also Psalms 9, 18 and 36.

3. See also Psalms 90 and 92. Life is very safe for many of us who live in a well-off, law-abiding welfare state with access to reliable technology. We can easily take advantage of this and assume we can do whatever we wish. James 4:3–15 reminds us that our lives are in God's hands and although we may plan, those plans should be qualified by, 'if the Lord wills'. We are vaporous mortals in the vast sweep of human history, let alone eternity.

4. See also Psalms 48, 87 and 122. The Church gets a lot of stick, much of it deserved. However, it is also God's instrument and demonstration of salvation. No other organisation matches it for its mercy ministry across the globe. Instead of merely bemoaning our failures, let's celebrate this Bride of Christ who daily prepares herself by service for the day of consummation (Rev. 19:8).

5. See also Psalms 114 and 126. Reflection on our personal history and the Lord's saving work in our lives often evokes gratitude in our hearts. None of us deserved saving; it is all by grace. Every believer is a divine story in the writing. It is good to share these tales with one another for encouragement. Try to let everyone have equal opportunity to speak.

6. See also Psalms 78 and 113. Newer churches often lack a sense of history; others might get stuck in it. However, the bulk of the Bible is a record of divine history. It is

recorded for our instruction, caution and encouragement. This is why it's helpful read the Old Testament as well as the New Testament. We also need to familiarise ourselves with church history, and the lives of godly pioneers.

7. See also Psalms 63, 103 and 145. This final Discussion Starter is designed to encourage us to contemplate the Lord's blessings in our lives. These are many and varied and inspires thanksgiving. You could read the Personal Application as a lead-in to help group members review their lifestyles in connection with contemplative practices and frequency. What are the hindrances and distractions? What is the best time and place? Any suggestions as to what works for each of us?

To conclude, after reading the Seeing Jesus in the Scriptures section, have some prayer for this to prove fruitful in our lives over the long term. Let it not be a duty but a daily delight, as Jesus Himself found it to be.

Enhanced reading: Psalm 8; 9; 18; 19; 29; 36; 39; 48; 63; 65; 76; 78; 84; 87; 90; 92; 93; 97; 103; 104; 105; 113; 114; 122; 126; 139; 144; 145.

Week Seven: Psalms of Adoration

Focus: Our calling is to praise the Lord at all times, in all places and all circumstances.

Opening Icebreaker

The icebreaker is simply to orientate us as to the 'why' of worship.

Discussion Starters

1. See also Psalms 67 and 117. This is to emphasise the holistic nature of celebrating God's mercy. He has healed us, raised us to life. We can praise God for His short-lived anger and lifelong favour. Night-time tears give way to morning joy. He turns our mourning into dancing. Our souls rejoice and won't be silent. We can thank Him forever and praise Him for His good government and abundant provision. Praise the Lord, worldwide; His kindness never ends and His truth lasts forever.

2. See also Psalms 108 and 135. Fervency, enthusiasm, passion and noise characterise these psalms. Heaven is not a quiet place, except for a recorded half hour (Rev. 8:1). Instead it is a place of dynamic, all-embracing, all-consuming activity. Jesus really has won! When a conquering Roman general returned home, the city turned out to do justice to his achievements. So let's not offer desultory routine in place of real celebration. How does our worship compare to the enthusiastic roar of heaven in Revelation 5:9–14?

3. See also Psalm 66. Victory for God's people might include thanksgiving for restored health or emerging from other difficulties for which we have pleaded for help and deliverance. Let us not forget that many thousands are persecuted every day for their faith, but also that the Lord delivers many thousands, as well. Take note of these things and rejoice with those who have found victory and deliverance, while weeping for those still struggling.

4. Christian magazines, newsletters and websites (such as tearfund.org and uspg.org.uk) are great tools for learning about how organisations are spreading the gospel worldwide. You could support them by praying for them

and giving thanks for the many long-term and short-term missions around the world.

5. The day of judgment is often perceived as a fearful threat and a subject that we don't like to talk about. However, in the psalms it is viewed with anticipation and relief as the time when God rights all the wrongs, deals with all evil people who abuse the poor, weak and vulnerable, and liberates the oppressed. Believers are already delivered from judgment through Christ; we should rejoice that He rules the renegade nations with a rod of iron. See also Psalms 96, 99, 138 and 149.

6. See also Psalms 95, 98 and 148. Some churches seem more rooted in God's works of creation; others appear totally shut into the doctrines of salvation. Christ is the Lord of both. Remember that He is the Lord of concrete and plastic and not just of trees and flowers. Let everything praise the Lord! Our theology needs to be rooted in the totality of His upholding the universe by His word of power – creation and redemption alike are expressions of His love and grace for which we give thanks.

7. See also Psalm 134. Church in the New Testament always refers to people and never to buildings. Nonetheless, although Jesus dispensed with all sacred 'hills' of worship, the temple metaphor is used of heaven's eternal temple to which all His people gather to worship (see Heb. 12:22–24).

Read the Personal Application. You might as a group wish to compose an antiphonal psalm using the 'His love endures for ever' response, but writing your own contemporary reasons why we give thanks. This could make a good song. Equally, you could write your own privately. Finally, read

the Seeing Jesus in the Scriptures section just to remind the group that Jesus worshipped on earth and is, as our great high priest, still our worship leader.

Enhanced reading: Psalm 30; 47; 66; 67; 68; 75; 95; 96; 98; 99; 100; 108; 117; 134; 135; 136; 138; 147; 148; 149; 150.

Notes...

The *Cover to Cover* Bible Study Series

1 Corinthians
Growing a Spirit-filled church
ISBN: 978-1-85345-374-8

2 Corinthians
Restoring harmony
ISBN: 978-1-85345-551-3

1,2,3 John
Walking in the truth
ISBN: 978-1-78259-763-6

1 Peter
Good reasons for hope
ISBN: 978-1-78259-088-0

2 Peter
*Living in the light of God's
promises*
ISBN: 978-1-78259-403-1

23rd Psalm
The Lord is my shepherd
ISBN: 978-1-85345-449-3

1 Timothy
*Healthy churches – effective
Christians*
ISBN: 978-1-85345-291-8

2 Timothy and Titus
Vital Christianity
ISBN: 978-1-85345-338-0

Abraham
Adventures of faith
ISBN: 978-1-78259-089-7

Acts 1–12
Church on the move
ISBN: 978-1-85345-574-2

Acts 13–28
To the ends of the earth
ISBN: 978-1-85345-592-6

Barnabas
Son of encouragement
ISBN: 978-1-85345-911-5

Bible Genres
Hearing what the Bible really says
ISBN: 978-1-85345-987-0

Daniel
Living boldly for God
ISBN: 978-1-85345-986-3

David
A man after God's own heart
ISBN: 978-1-78259-444-4

Ecclesiastes
*Hard questions and spiritual
answers*
ISBN: 978-1-85345-371-7

Elijah
A man and his God
ISBN: 978-1-85345-575-9

Elisha
A lesson in faithfulness
ISBN: 978-1-78259-494-9

Ephesians
Claiming your inheritance
ISBN: 978-1-85345-229-1

Esther
For such a time as this
ISBN: 978-1-85345-511-7

Ezekiel
A prophet for all times
ISBN: 978-1-78259-836-7

Fruit of the Spirit
Growing more like Jesus
ISBN: 978-1-85345-375-5

Galatians
Freedom in Christ
ISBN: 978-1-85345-648-0

Genesis 1–11
Foundations of reality
ISBN: 978-1-85345-404-2

Genesis 12–50
Founding fathers of faith
ISBN: 978-1-78259-960-9

God's Rescue Plan
*Finding God's fingerprints on
human history*
ISBN: 978-1-85345-294-9

Great Prayers of the Bible
Applying them to our lives today
ISBN: 978-1-85345-253-6

Habakkuk
Choosing God's way
ISBN: 978-1-78259-843-5

Haggai
Motivating God's people
ISBN: 978-1-78259-686-8

Hebrews
Jesus – simply the best
ISBN: 978-1-85345-337-3

Isaiah 1–39
Prophet to the nations
ISBN: 978-1-85345-510-0

Isaiah 40–66
Prophet of restoration
ISBN: 978-1-85345-550-6

Jacob
Taking hold of God's blessing
ISBN: 978-1-78259-685-1

James
Faith in action
ISBN: 978-1-85345-293-2

Jeremiah
The passionate prophet
ISBN: 978-1-85345-372-4

Job
The source of wisdom
ISBN: 978-1-78259-992-0

Joel
Getting real with God
ISBN: 978-1-78951-927-2

John's Gospel
Exploring the seven miraculous signs
ISBN: 978-1-85345-295-6

Jonah
Rescued from the depths
ISBN: 978-1-78259-762-9

Joseph
The power of forgiveness and reconciliation
ISBN: 978-1-85345-252-9

Joshua 1–10
Hand in hand with God
ISBN: 978-1-85345-542-7

Joshua 11–24
Called to service
ISBN: 978-1-78951-138-3

Judges 1–8
The spiral of faith
ISBN: 978-1-85345-681-7

Judges 9–21
Learning to live God's way
ISBN: 978-1-85345-910-8

Luke
A prescription for living
ISBN: 978-1-78259-270-9

Mark
Life as it is meant to be lived
ISBN: 978-1-85345-233-8

Mary
The mother of Jesus
ISBN: 978-1-78259-402-4

Moses
Face to face with God
ISBN: 978-1-85345-336-6

Names of God
Exploring the depths of God's character
ISBN: 978-1-85345-680-0

Nehemiah
Principles for life
ISBN: 978-1-85345-335-9

Parables
Communicating God on earth
ISBN: 978-1-85345-340-3

Philemon
From slavery to freedom
ISBN: 978-1-85345-453-0

Philippians
Living for the sake of the gospel
ISBN: 978-1-85345-421-9

Prayers of Jesus
Hearing His heartbeat
ISBN: 978-1-85345-647-3

Proverbs
Living a life of wisdom
ISBN: 978-1-85345-373-1

Psalms
Songs of life
ISBN: 978-1-78951-240-3

Revelation 1–3
Christ's call to the Church
ISBN: 978-1-85345-461-5

Revelation 4–22
The Lamb wins! Christ's final victory
ISBN: 978-1-85345-411-0

Rivers of Justice
Responding to God's call to righteousness today
ISBN: 978-1-85345-339-7

Ruth
Loving kindness in action
ISBN: 978-1-85345-231-4

Song of Songs
A celebration of love
ISBN: 978-1-78259-959-3

The Armour of God
Living in His strength
ISBN: 978-1-78259-583-0

The Beatitudes
Immersed in the grace of Christ
ISBN: 978-1-78259-495-6

The Creed
Belief in action
ISBN: 978-1-78259-202-0

The Divine Blueprint
God's extraordinary power in ordinary lives
ISBN: 978-1-85345-292-5

The Holy Spirit
Understanding and experiencing Him
ISBN: 978-1-85345-254-3

The Image of God
His attributes and character
ISBN: 978-1-85345-228-4

The Kingdom
Studies from Matthew's Gospel
ISBN: 978-1-85345-251-2

The Letter to the Colossians
In Christ alone
ISBN: 978-1-855345-405-9

The Letter to the Romans
Good news for everyone
ISBN: 978-1-85345-250-5

The Lord's Prayer
Praying Jesus' way
ISBN: 978-1-85345-460-8

The Prodigal Son
Amazing grace
ISBN: 978-1-85345-412-7

The Second Coming
Living in the light of Jesus' return
ISBN: 978-1-85345-422-6

The Sermon on the Mount
Life within the new covenant
ISBN: 978-1-85345-370-0

Thessalonians
Building Church in changing times
ISBN: 978-1-78259-443-7

The Ten Commandments
Living God's Way
ISBN: 978-1-85345-593-3

The Uniqueness of our Faith
What makes Christianity distinctive?
ISBN: 978-1-85345-232-1

Courses and events

Waverley Abbey College

Publishing and media

Conference facilities

Transforming lives

CWR's vision is to enable people to experience personal transformation through applying God's Word to their lives and relationships.

Our Bible-based training and resources help people around the world to:
• Grow in their walk with God
• Understand and apply Scripture to their lives
• Resource themselves and their church
• Develop pastoral care and counselling skills
• Train for leadership
• Strengthen relationships, marriage and family life and much more.

Our insightful writers provide daily Bible reading notes and other resources for all ages, and our experienced course designers and presenters have gained an international reputation for excellence and effectiveness.

CWR's Training and Conference Centre in Surrey, England, provides excellent facilities in an idyllic setting – ideal for both learning and spiritual refreshment.

CWR Applying God's Word
to everyday life and relationships

CWR, Waverley Abbey House,
Waverley Lane, Farnham,
Surrey GU9 8EP, UK

Telephone: **+44 (0)1252 784700**
Email: **info@cwr.org.uk**
Website: **cwr.org.uk**

Registered Charity No. 294387
Company Registration No. 1990308